Alf - That's All Jokes

Written by Chris Leworthy

Copyright © 2021 Chris Leworthy

All rights reserved.

ISBN: 9798514692095

DEDICATION

A huge thank you to my wife Laurie for putting up with my endless jokes, to my parents, to all the friends i've made since starting comedy in 2015 who have encouraged me all the way and to everyone who follows me online and takes their time to interact, this is for you.

FOREWORD

So in May 2021 I decided I should write a Joke Book, the working title for it was "Blindfolded Archery and Other Jokes I wished I'd never written" as Blindfolded Archery seems to be a topic I keep going back to.

Of all the names being considered it was that one that stuck in my head.

I told my Brother and he said "Who exactly would it be aimed at?".

I told my Dad (Daz) and he said "I can't see a Target audience for it"

Even my Proof-reader said "Some of the Jokes are a little wide of the mark"

Personally I couldn't see a problem but decided to call it 'That's All Jokes'.

I hope you enjoy it and it makes you laugh, either out loud or to yourself, both are fine.

Any typos are there on purpose as a kind of 'Wheres Wally' side quest for my pedantic twitter followers.

@whoelsebutalf on Twitter

◆ ◆ ◆

JOKES

1.

If you've never tried blindfolded Archery,
you don't know what you are missing.

2.

I went on an activity weekend with my Wife.
She got to try out Blindfolded Archery and all
I got was a bloody T-shirt.

3.

My medical condition means I can
smell coconut from 10mtrs away.
Which was really helpful at my first
job because I was a Bounty hunter.

4.

When I split up with my last Girlfriend she kept
all my Kevin Bacon films and small french cakes.
But on the plus side, I am now Footloose
& Fancy free.

5.

I've got a pet Panda called 'Little Richard'.
He eats A Wop Bop A Loo Bop A Lot of Bamboo.

6.

When I told my wife that I thought her Praying Mantis
fancy dress outfit was unrealistic, she bit my head off.

7.

The White twins were in my school year, we
nicknamed them White Lightning and White Spirit.
They looked almost identical but
White Spirit was Thinner.

8.

I was in a stationery shop the other day
when I got hit on the head by a wrench.
Someone's always got to go and
throw a spanner in The Works.

9.

A man just cycled past me with no arms.
I don't know his name but his face rung a bell.

10.

I used to be in a Band called 'The Dead Badgers'.
We just played middle of the road type stuff.

11.

Currently listening to an Audiobook
called 'Thinking the Unthinkable',
Chris Eubank tells the story of The Titanic.

12.

I got 3 calls from the lady at Wicks today
saying the red taps I ordered are now in stock.
I think she's got the Hots for me.

13.

I won £150 playing Poker online.
Best £500 I ever spent.

14.

Just watching Kill Bill Volume 2.
I had to put the subtitles on as it was so quiet.

15.

I've just run out of Dark Crayons.
Completely out of the Blue.

16.

My Facebook stalker died recently.

I wont be seeing the likes of him anymore.

17.

I can't believe my place of work took way the Suggestion Box. Still, can't complain.

18.

My no-nonsense approach to work is the reason I lost my job as a Clown.

19.

When I was 18, I used to wash Saucers for a living.

I loved working at Area 51.

20.

My Redundancy joke may seem quite long.

But it's worth it for the payoff.

"I'm a senior member of the Clowning Association"

A bigwig?

Yeah and a red nose

22.

When I was younger, my school was
located in a model village.
I had trouble fitting in.

23.

My School was sponsored by Ikea.
So assembly took ages.

24.

Growing up we didn't have a lot of money.
I had to use a hand-me-down
calculator with no multiplication symbol on it.
Times were hard.

25.

I didn't despise GCSE Chemistry,
just certain elements.

26.

I'm hiding in my Finnish neighbour's shed,
waiting to jump out and surprise him.
It's like a sauna in here.

27.

My boss came home from work early
and found me and his wife in the Jacuzzi.
I'm in Hot Water now.

28.

Why do I think my wife left me?
Well, because I tried installing a
Hot Tub in her summerhouse.
That was the water shed moment.

29.

Someone just showed me a photo of a heated reservoir.
Hot Dam!!

> 'ENTER NEW PASSWORD'

~ 'CHICKEN'

> 'PASSWORD MUST CONTAIN A CAPITAL'

~ 'CHICKENKIEV'

31.
When I was young I was adopted by a man called Daz,
he was my non-biological father.

32.
My parents abandoned me at a young age
because of my obsession with paddles.
I grew up an Oar-fan.

33.
My Dad's got no left arm,
he bought me up single handedly

34.
Which was a challenge because
as a child I was a right handful.

35.
My Dad always used to leave Church
before any of the singing started.
As did his father before hymns.

36.

I visit my Uncle once a month to
help him apply his fake tan.
I'm like the 'Sun He Never Had'.

37.

I've got a Conjoined Uncle.
On my Father's side.

38.

My Uncle was a journalist when he came
up with the Yank-my-Finger and Fart prank.
Shortly after that he won the Pull-it-surprise.

39.
I filled my Uncle's inhaler with nitrous oxide.
I thought he'd be mad, but he laughed it off.

40.
My Grandad was meant to be Kennedy's bodyguard on November 22nd 1963 but called in sick.
Really dodged a bullet that day.

41.
Mr Gran recently died in Quick Sand.
Still hasn't quite sunk in.

42.
I love winding up old people.
I went to see Grandad recently and he's had a catheter fitted.
I had to take the piss out of it.

43.
I always wanted to be a professional wrestler like my Grandad.
He always wanted to be a professional wrestler too.

44.

My Brother hasn't spoken to anyone
about his obsession for home-brewing.
He just tends to bottle it up.

45.

My Brother goes to the All-You-Can-Eat
Buffet when he's stressed.
He's got a lot on his plate at the moment.

46.

My Brother jumped out at me while I was
carrying my James Bond DVD collection down the stairs.
He scared The Living Daylights out of me.

47.

My Brother spent many years working
for Adobe, and then one day he just quit unexpectedly.

48.

My lasting childhood memory was
my brother poking a twig in my ear.
Sticks in the mind.

49.
My Brother is always super competitive,
i've just got a new
dog called Terry and he's now gone
and got one that is apparently 'Terrier'.

50.
My Brother got fired from his job at the brewery.
In fairness, he was wasted at that job.

51.
My sister had a real problem with drink
before she started up her upholstery business.
Now she's a recovering alcoholic.

52.
My cousin is an Alanis Morissette tribute act
who doesnt perform her biggest hit.
Which is Ironic.

53.
My sister often gets in to fights in the
nightclub cloakroom.
I say fight, it's mainly just handbags.

54.

When my brother is stressed he sniffs glue.

It's the only thing that's holding him together right now.

55.

My cousin turned up at our wedding

reception wearing stilettos.

Danced for 5 minutes

Broke both her shoe heels

and left shortly after.

56.

Making alterations to people's trousers.

That's something I've recently taken up.

57.

Would I recommend a job at the Dulux paint factory?

I've got mixed emulsions.

58.

I quit my last job without making a scene.

I was a terrible set designer.

59.

I got fired from Alton Towers on tuesday
and started a new job at Thorpe Park
on thursday, it's been a rollercoaster few days.

60.

I've threatened my boss that i'm going to
turn up to work wearing a fake moustache,
but i'm having trouble making it stick.

61.

I got a lift to work this morning.
I'm a pretty good elevator engineer.

62.

I used to wash dishes for a living. Now my work is drying up.

63.

My co-worker is a shotputter.
He's always throwing his weight around.

Do you want to go to the casino at the highest point in China?

Tibet?

Well what else do you expect us to be doing there

65.

My dad left when I was 5 to go and buy some camouflage clothing and never returned.

At least.... i don't think he came back.

66.

My dad once had dinner with William G Stewart, it was at 12:45.

Or as he used to say "15 to 1".

67.

How come when a dog licks it's privates in public, its OK, but when my father did it he got thrown out of the Army.

68.

Injured myself on dad's record collection last night.

A Madness album fell off the shelf

and hit me on the head.

I've got the ska to prove it.

69.

At grandad's funeral we decided to bury him vertically.

Plot twist.

70.

My grandad use to have a saying;

"You've got to take the Rough with the Smooth".

The best sandpaper salesman I've ever met.

71.

Even though it has no working brake lights, my 90 year old grandad still drives his car to work everyday. Still no sign of him slowing down.

72.

We had a new student come in to school once, who was covered head to toe in temporary tattoos. He was a transfer student.

73.

My girlfriend pressured me into getting a tattoo on my calf.
Now i'm in a lot of trouble with the RSPCA.

74.

My mate told me he'd accidentally slit his wrist whilst opening a jar of mayonnaise.
I was like "bloody Hellman!"

JOKE FROM THE BAKERY

> I would like a sweet pastry please

> Danish

> Oh Sorry, Jeg vil gerne have et sødt kager venligst

ADVERTS

Yoga Instructor required.

Flexible working hours.

Dictionary for Sale.

Brand New, Never Opened, Hardback, Dinosaur, Bacon.

These are all words that are in it.

Wrestling Move of the Year.

Now accepting Submissions.

ADVERTS

To Rent.

Full suit of Armour.

Available for one knight.

Available: Goat Farmer looking for Work

Great with Kids.

For Sale

Broken Limbo Dancing equipment.

10 pounds won't go any lower.

82.

Sad News

My obese parrot died today.

It is however, a huge weight off my shoulders.

83.

It's only recently that I've realised

how much crap there is on the TV.

I'm gonna have to keep my parrot in a cage from now on.

84.

I've just adopted a homing pigeon,

but I can't remember it's name.

I'm sure it'll come back to me though.

85.

Sent my dead duck away to be cremated.

Just received his ashes in the post

along with the bill.

86.

All of my gun dogs keep running away, so if anyone

can give me some pointers.

87.

Someone just asked me if I wanted to come to their rabbit pampering party tonight.

I mean, I'd love to go but I'm washing my Hare.

88.

I'm making my baby lamb live outside.

I can't wrap him in cotton wool his whole life.

89.

Unfortunately my horse Toto couldn't race today.

I left his reins down in Africa.

90.

Chameleons are meant to blend well

but I think it's ruined this smoothie.

91.

I asked my german mate:
"When you spell 'Dog' in german,
does it contain the letter K?"
He said "K? Nein".

92.

People are already congratulating me for
cross breeding a wildebeest and a cheetah.
Gnus travels fast around here.

93.

Trying to write another funny joke
about giving helium to my sheep, but i'm
worried that I may have set the baa too high.

ALF'S CRUMBLY FRUITCAKE TOUR

MORE DATES WILL BE ADDED SOON

If you haven't seen me on my Crumbly Fruitcake Tour, more dates will be added soon.

95.

The Window Cleaning World
Championships had to be put on hold.
There was a streaker.

96.

Is there still a possibility that the
KerPlunk World Championships
won't be cancelled, or am I just clutching at straws.

97.

I came 4th in the Lego Model
Dismantling World Championships.
It's not about the winning though,
it's the taking apart.

98.

I've never been to a casino myself, but my
brother made most of his fortune by counting cards.
He was in charge of stocktaking at Clinton's.

99.

It's easier to get a bank loan first thing in the morning.

Come on, credit where it's dew.

100.

Just found a piece of Scalextric in my coat pocket.

I think someone is trying to keep track on me.

101.

Someone put superglue on my paintballing gloves.

My mates keep telling me to throw

them away but I'm sticking to my guns.

102.

I think someone's been watering down

my whiskey but I don't have the Proof.

103.

I always keep emergency flares in my car boot.

You never know when you might

get invoted to a 70's themed disco.

104.

Vincent Van Gogh had a terrific memory.

Everything you told him went in one ear..

105.

No one warned me about the

dangers of freezing protein powder.

I had to find out the hard whey.

Every household in our village nominates one
family member whose task it is to provide a
drawing of where they keep
their pants for a competition.
This year I've drawn the shorts drawer.

107.

There was a spider on the urinal

at Wetherspoons the other day.

I wasn't particularly bothered

about it but he was pissed off.

108.

I got invited to a slumber Party organised by my

'Bed Wetters Support Group'. I went in my pyjamas.

109.

My plumber accidentally hooked our

boiler up to our toilet and we didn't notice.

A few weeks later I started getting hot flushes.

110.

As I'm quickly running out of toilet paper,

I've decided to take a leaf out of Bear Grylls' book.

The library aren't going to be happy about it though.

111.

I was in my garden and next to my strawberry patch

was the front part off a Ford Fiesta.

Must be a bumper crop this year.

112.

When lockdown is over i'm looking forward to seeing

My Family and Friends.

In fact I'll happily watch any sitcom.

113.

Do you believe in Telepathy?

I would love to hear your thoughts.

30 years ago my Dad did painted a mural on the side of our house of one of the stars of Bonnie and Clyde.

Faye Dunaway?

Yeah, it's barely even visible any more.

115.
I hear Fleetwood Mac are releasing remastered albums later this year.
Probably just Rumours though.

116.
Someone stole my luggage which had pictures of Sting & Andy Summers on it.
Thankfully though, The Police are on the case.

117.
My new Cat is called 'Flashdance'.
What a Feline!

118.
The courtesy car I've been given has a CD multi changer with a Michael Jackson album and a Bee Gees single in it.
My ride home has just gone from 'Bad' to 'Words'.

119.

I asked George Michael what his
favourite type of biscuit was.
He said "Well, I guess it would be Nice".

120.

Busy day so far trying to put my
mediocre english rock cds in alphabetical order.
I'm up to my Elbows.

121.

I'm gonna spend today in a dinghy just
singing John Lennon songs.
Canoe imagine?

122.

Back in roman times, Little Mix
were know as 'Little 1,009'.

123.

My wife was once in a car crash with
someone called Kevin Fearnley-Whittingstall
and for that reason alone, I'll never watch River Cottage.
Although I shouldn't judge a cook by his brother.

124.

Thank you for calling the Brian Blessed Impressionist Hotline.
We are currently receiving high volume calls.

125.

I've just tried emailing Mackenzie Crook, but got
a message back saying he was 'Out of The Office'.
Come on mate that was 15 yrs ago,
stop banging on about it.

126.

I hear that the Arctic Monkeys recently sold
a carpet to the former Real Madrid manager.
I bet that it looks good on Zidane's floor.

127.

Just when you thought things couldn't
get any worse, someone's just Bought me
a teapot in the shape of Prince Charles.
It never reigns, it pours.

128.

Since my brother started collecting Kathy Bates
films on DVD, I've bought him nothing but Misery.

> **Have you heard about Roger Daltrey?**

> **Who's Roger Daltrey?**

> **Yep, that's the guy.**

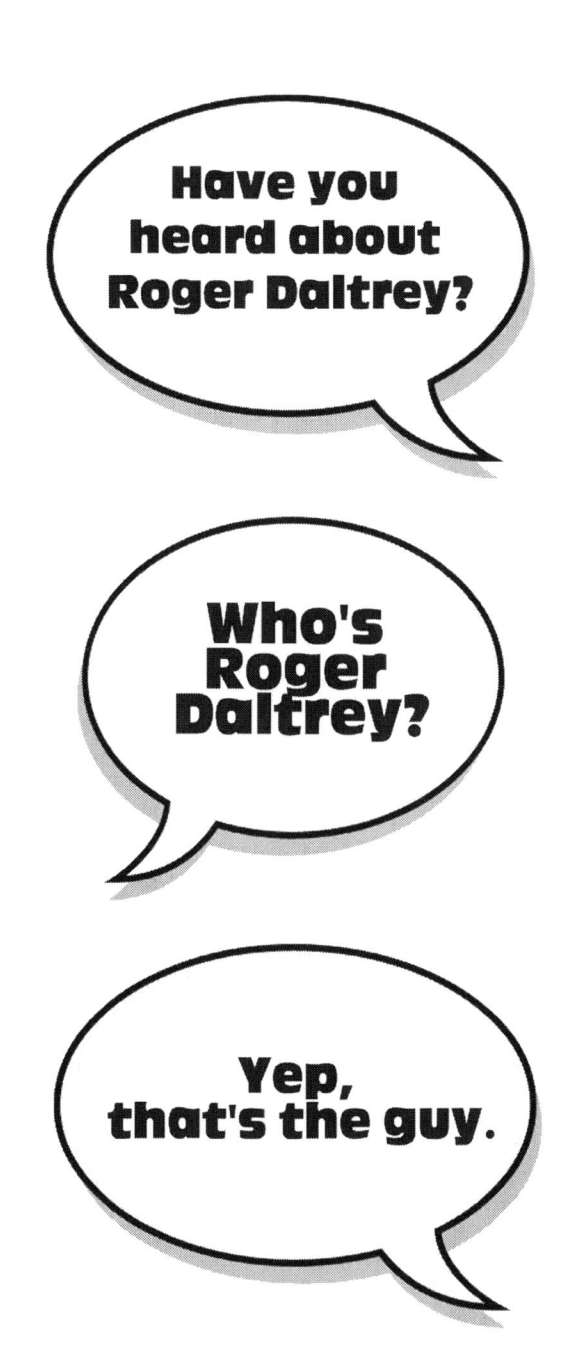

130.

I have a strange liking for Hugh Grant films.
I think it's more than a fondness,
it could be Love Actually.

131.

Sean Connery couldn't believe what he
had found in the back of his washing machine.
It was a shock.

132.

I'm just getting dressed up as
Christopher Robin to go to a fancy dress party.
Bear with me.

133.

I bought myself a 6ft Boomerang with
Characters from The Hobbit on it.
It's really hard to Frodo.

134.

So far today I've watched the 'Extended Version'
and the 'Directors Cut' of the latest Stephen King film.
That's the long and the short of It.

135.

I went for a walk on the moors
with the cast of Ghostbusters.
We didn't get very far though because
we weren't allowed to cross the Streams.

136.

I need to brush up on my film knowledge for a quiz so
I've been reading the 'A to Z of Keanu Reeves films'
for the past 3 weeks and I'm still not up to Speed.

137.

I skipped maths class so many
times at school, I can't even count.

138.

The inventor of the cliffhanger died today.
His funeral will be..

139.

I used to have a 3rd nipple.
It feels good to get that off my chest.

140.

I was recently voted the World's Worst Secret Keeper.....
but don't tell anyone.

141.

My mate just told me that his favourite hobby is hiding in tumble dryers.
I'm not quite sure how he got in to it.

142.

"My mate is still unable to re-open his shop because of all the Red Tape".
"Sorry to hear that, what does he do?"
"He's an unsuccessful Red Tape salesman".

143.

Me and my mate stole alot of 80's rock albums

from our local zoo.

I didn't keep all of them, but I did get the Lion's Cher.

> 'ENTER NEW PASSWORD'

~ 'BADUM'

> 'PASSWORD MUST CONTAIN A CYMBAL'

~ 'BADUMTSSS'

145.

When I found out that all my Judo classes
for the next month had been cancelled.

I flipped.

146.

Just cancelled my gym membership.

Wasn't working out.

147.

Got stuck at Slimming World for 3 days.

I could find the weigh In, but I couldn't find the way out.

148.

My online tapestry course

homework is due in by the weekend.

The deadline is looming.

149.

I've been a fan of gazpacho soup since before it was cool.

150.

I can still remember the time I

undercooked my french bread.

The pain is still raw.

151.

Spent all morning working in the garden,

ate 4 packs of Bacon flavored crisps

and now feeling Frazzled.

152.

Just making the final preparations

for this years 'National Jelly Awards'

The stage is set.

Mansell & Vettel

> How do you get your coffee table so shiny?

> Polish!

> Oh sorry, Jak sprawić, by Twój stolik był tak błyszczący?

155.

I'm just painting the hooks beside my front door.
Could probably do with another coat.

156.

I was born in a bungalow and lived there ever since.
Storey of my Life.

157.

My cleaner doesn't do the dusting anymore.
I don't want to say anything though,
because last time I mentioned it
she lost her rag.

158.

I've arranged for my driving instructor to arrive
at midnight and teach me how to do reverse parking.
It's probably too late to back out of it now though.

159.

I ran into an old school friend earlier today.

Which was nice, but did mean I failed my driving test.

160.

I've recently put a sticker on my car

that says 'Harry Kills Voldemort'.

But apparently that's not what my brother

meant about putting a Spoiler on my car.

161.

I've been so busy lately that my hobby of stealing fixtures

from peoples cars has had to take a back seat.

162.

I've been to escapology classes every day

for the past couple of months.

I think I need to get out more.

163.

I started up an evening support group for pessimists.

It was tough going, at first the class was half empty but

by the time I finished the class was half full.

164.

I went to my first Narcolepsy support group today.
It was so boring I almost fell asleep.

165.

Someone once described me as giving
terribly timed high fives.
That was a slap in the face.

166.

Just finished the Christmas grocery shop, it went
well and then right at the end I bought some
marzipan which was the icing on the cake.

167.

Unfortunately I can't make to the Christmas Party
for Flat Earthers in New Zealand this year,
but it's not the end of the world... or is it

168.

I'm so fanatical about football that I spent
my Christmas bonus on a VAR system.
My wife isn't happy, she says I've crossed the line.
We'll see about that.

169.

Someone stole all my lightbulbs, not
sure who it was though.
I'm completely in the dark.

170.

I once drove from Newcastle to Truro and only
had to look at a map once, as I arrived in Edinburgh.

171.

At school I was a member of the Reminiscing Club.
And even to this day it still brings back fond memories...

172.

Someone stole the ruler I've had for 20 years.
The disappointment I feel is immeasurable.

173.
I was recently voted Dental Hygenist of the Year.
All I got for though was a little plaque.

174.
I spent a lot of my childhood at a correctional facility.
I worked saturdays at the Tippex factory.

175.
I've grown a handlebar moustache,
but it's made my bike look stupid.

176.
I was at the funeral for the CEO of Optrex.
Very sad, not a dry eye in the house.

On a lighter note

178.

I put all my time and money into

my new crab fishing business.

And unfortunately now i'm starting to feel the pinch.

179.

Just off to eskimo speed dating.

I've come up with an excellent ice breaker.

180.

Learning to play Wonderwall on the panpipes.

I'm hoping to create an Oasis of calm.

181.

Just found out the house I bought has a haunted loft.

That's problem-attic.

182.

The apprentice at my local Fishmongers quit today.

They're looking for someone to take his plaice.

183.

I'm playing cricket against a team from
my local Fish & Chip shop this afternoon.
Their fielders and bowler aren't that good,
but their batter's brilliant.

184.

Just bought myself a new hawaiian shirt.
All the ham & pineapple had fallen off my last one.

185.

Just bought some potatoes to have for
my tea from a town in Wiltshire.
Chippenham?
No I thought I'd do them as wedges.

"Just got a new apartment in a block of flats in South Wales."

"Tenby?"

"No, 22A."

187.

The local council have just announced
where they're building a new reservoir.
It's not the location I suggested
though which was a dam site better.

188.

He's already a green belt and
he's still looking to build on it.

189.

My wife recently told me that she
wanted to learn to drive a steam roller.
I said "I'm not going to stand in your way"

190.

Why did I apply for the steam roller drivers job?
Well, I'm gonna level with you.

191.

I'm so stressed, I might go potholing.

I tend to cave under pressure.

192.

Some guy just knocked at my house and
tried to sell me a golden door handle for £5000.

What a knob.

193.

I didn't perform very well at the

San Andreas Tennis Open.

Too many faults.

194.

My company that makes 'Driveways for Pubs'

took a while to get going.

But finally, I seem to be making inn roads.

WRONG
WRONG WRONG
WRONG WRONG
WRONG WRONG WRONG
WRONG
WRONG WRONG
WRONG

What've I been up to today? Just writing a few wrongs.

196.
Someone offered me a free gate.
I said "What's the Catch?"
He said "It's the bit that allows
it to open and close".

197.
If any one wants to buy any of
my chiropractor magazines off me.
I've got plenty of back issues.

198.
Writing a school nativity is very easy.
In fact it's childs play.

199.
I asked my Mum what she
keeps in the car boot,
and she went Spare!

200.
My wife didn't want me to enter us
in the Chinese Burn competition.
But eventually I twisted her arm.

201.

I just hope that I never get arthritis in my hand.
Fingers Crossed.

202.

For my birthday, my wife bought me a ticket to go to the Giant Clock Museum in Davenport, USA.
Iowa, big time.

203.

The best photos of potato waffles are those taken from a Birdseye view.

204.

The issue of blank envelopes.

This needs addressing!!!!

205.

I entered an Astronomy competition.

I came in 2nd and won an awesome map of the stars.

Not a bad constellation Prize.

206.

Just hanging a giant periodic table on the wall.

I'm only using 1 nail though,

just to add the element of danger.

207.

10 passengers today who's called

me a Terrible Bus Driver.

I don't know where these people get off.

208.

If I can't sleep, I like to fill my bath with coffee.
Then I fall asleep in an instant.

209.

I couldn't sleep last night, so I went down to
the beach with my dinghy and I soon drifted off.

210.

Just watching a TV show about a lazy ironmonger.
It's very poorly cast.

211.

I've got a reputation as a rubbish babysitter.
I don't mind.

"What do we want?"

Less punchlines and More Car Noises

"When do we want it?"

Neeeeeeoooooooowwwww

213.

I've spent so much money on mini battenburgs,
I've been left with Kipling debt.

214.

I built a snooker table using all my old school books.
Math books for cloth, English books for the cues.....
and the rest is History.

215.

My local baker is pretty speedy.
He made me an Apple Cake from
scratch in under 2 minutes,
which you have to admit, is a quick turnover.

216.

My mate was put in to a coma
by thieves who stole his castanets.
He looks set to make a Maraca-less recovery.

217.

Bad news about that kid who swallowed a spanner.

Gut-Wrenching.

218.

Really shouldn't have started a fight with the
Pirate at our local pantomime.
He's got a tremendous left hook.

219.

I've just found out the Gobstopper factory
has closed and gone into administration.
Honestly, I'm finding it a little hard to swallow.

VISITING MY LOCAL GP

> I think you may have Pneumonoultramicroscopic-silicovolcanoconiosis.

> What are the Symptoms?

> It's hard to say.

221.
It may be pronounced
'Milled Wholegrain Wheat'
but it's actually spelt flour.

222.
Just finished browsing the revamped
webpage 'www.HiveKeepers.com'.
It really is a site to Bee hold.

223.
After his ark idea was over, Noah organised a safari trip.
The animals went in 4 x 4s.

224.
I'm very close to finishing Sherlock's yoga DVD,
I'm on the Holmes stretch.

225.
As a leaving present from my first job
they gave me a cheese slicer.
Since then I've gone onto grate things.

226.
People tell me the way I make rice pudding is dreadful.
I'm not worried, I've got thick skin.

227.
Over the last week I've been recruiting &
training well mannered children to steal yoghurts.
And i'm proud to say, the gang is
starting to take shape nicely.

228.
Off to university in an attempt to
improve my Cuppa Soup making technique.
I'm doing a Bachelors degree.

229.
The Doctor told me my high blood pressure
is due to all the sodium in my diet.
But I'm going to take that with a pinch of salt.

230.

My old chemistry teacher used to have

a Pb & J sandwich everyday.

He ended up dying from Lead poisoning.

231.

What's the best way to keep my hazelnuts,

nougat and caramel bars from melting in this weather.

That's today's Hot Topic.

232.

Should I release a Butterscotch flavoured Licquor.

Probably Werther shot.

"Took all my old Star Trek figurines to a car boot sale in the scottish borders."

"Selkirk?"

"Afraid not, but I got rid of Spock & Scotty."

234.

My mate rides his bike to work
everyday without wearing helmet.
I keep telling him one day he
might crash into a lamp post.
He still hasn't wrapped his head around it.

235.

My ex-girlfriend was a keen cyclist.
I used to follow her everywhere in the car.
In the end we broke up because I wasn't
giving her enough space.

236.

I stopped dating the girl from my local athletics club.
She was just giving me the run around.

237.

Tripped down the stairs at Gatwick once.
The injury wasn't too bad, just an airline fracture.

238.

I think my new years resolution for 2017

is going to be 'Stop living in the Past'.

239.

As a child, my dad caught me barbecueing

a wolf behind the garage,

so to punish me he made me smoke the whole pack.

240.

I recently got in troube for punching my Landlord.

I was just fed up with him walking

around like he owned the place.

241.

The trampoline at my local park has
been out of order since Sunday.
That's 3 days on the bounce.

242.

I've been listening to instrumental versions
of The Police songs.
It really takes the Sting out of them.

243.

Performing accapella versions of U2 songs.
That really seems to takes the Edge off.

244.

Gary Barlow just asked me if I wanted to cover for
Robbie Williams on his bands tour.
I don't know how to Take That.

245.

The lead singer of Steppenwolf
was known as Tobias Wilde.
What people don't realise is that
he was actually born Toby Wild.

246.

If you think about it, we're all obsessed
with Blondie lyrics in one way or another.

247.

I've written a joke about the song 'Kayleigh',
but just googled it and found it's been done a Marillion times before

248.

Just been watching that new documentary
about Mick Hucknall becoming a ploughman.
Simply Harrowing.

249.

People have started ridiculing me because my Erasure CD collection is still incomplete.

All i'm asking for is A Little Respect.

250.

I used to think that Aled Jones was a dead english singer.

But turns out he's alive and welsh.

251.

I met a girl online and suggested we go on a date to 'Somewhere Only we Know'.

She didn't turn up, maybe I was too Keane.

252.

Michael Jackson Albums....

They're not all Bad.

253.

Parking at Jim Henson studios is always a problem.
All the spaces are 'Kermit Holders only'.

254.

I asked my wife why she was upset
but she didn't want to talk about it.
I bet she's joined a fight club.

255.

Damn, my wife's just came home and found me
dancing around the house to one of her boy band CDs.
Busted!!

256.

I've just been doing the dishes dressed
as Dumbledore and my wife is doing the
Hoovering dressed as Hermione Granger.
Just your normal sunday, Pottering about the house.

257.

My ears are burning that means
someones talking about me.
They're probably saying something like
"Why's that idiot got his head in the oven".

258.

My Microwave has broken more
times than I've had hot dinners.

259.

I get a round of applause
everytime I try to cook my dinner.
I've got a fan oven.

260.

Accidentally dropped my
autobiography into a deep fat fryer.
I'm frittering my life away.

261.

Hello, is this the Eczema Sufferers Helpline?

Yes. Sorry, you're cracking up

262.

Thank you for calling the Wild Cat Chatline. All our Lions are currently busy..........

263.

It's not particularly warm in Argentina at the moment.
In fact, you could say it's bordering on Chile.

264.

How would I say my first year as a
pig farmer in the Himalayas has gone?
It's peaks and troughs.

265.

There's a small island off the coast of Italy
which is inhabited by 5 million Sicillion people.
That's the biggest number i've ever heard.

266.

Last year I wrote a joke about stockholm
syndrome which I didn't really like.
But over time it's something I've grown to love.

267.

Until I learned about Italics in school,

I was a straight A student.

268.

As a child I was too shy for the role of

'The Talking Rock' in our school play.

The teachers said I needed to be a little boulder.

269.

I got on very well with my Science teacher at School.

We had Chemistry.

270.

Our school production of 'Breaking Bad' has

8 different roles and we only have 5 actors.

You do the Meth.

271.

In Iceland it is illegal to walking your dog naked,

that also goes for Tesco and Asda.

272.

Proud to announce that for the 3rd year running,

the World Breath Holding Championship

went without a hiccup.

273.

I tried to go to the grand opening of local Bird Sanctuary.

But because I didn't have an invite,

they wouldn't let me in.

It was RSPB only.

274.

I dont want to let the cat out of the bag but

I'm currently in alot of trouble with the RSPCA.

275.

I think I may have added one

too many rooms to my house.

According to a recent study.

276.

I stayed in a Hobbit themed hotel once.

They were short staffed.

277.

Very busy on the high street today.

My local charity shop is selling clothes

like they're going out of fashion.

It's just a shame Salem will only ever be remembered for the trials.

Which trials?

Yeah, that's the ones.

279.

I've been reading a book called 'the A to Z of Fruit'.
I'm almost up to date.

280.

Just finished reading a book called 'The Amazing Basement'.
It's a best cellar.

281.

I was a bit disappointed with The Hunchback of Notre Dame 2.
I was hoping for more of Quasimodo's back story.

282.

I could have been a professional Monopoly player.
But I never got the chance.

283.

I've considered changing my name to 'Skip Intro',
so I can put on comedy posters 'As Seen On Netflix'.

284.

People don't realise that my real name is Lance.
It's not a common name now-a-days but in
medieval times people were called Lance-a-lot.

285.

I've achieved two things today:
1. I finished that Dot-to-Dot that i'd been meaning to do.
2. Angered my neighbour, by drawing
all over his Dalmation.

286.

I'm changing my last name to Shotgun.
I've always fancied a double-barrelled surname.

287.

Explosive Dough? That's the last thing I knead.

288.

My ex-girlfriend was heavily into feng shui and always
had to decorate each room herself.
But since she moved out the tables have turned.

289.

Dr Frankenstein is my favourite body builder.

290.

My girlfriend asked me why I never buy her jewelry.

I didn't even know she sold Jewelry.

291.

My last girlfriend was an auctioneer.

I love her lots.

292.

I think my new girlfriend is polish.

The first time we met she took an immediate shine to me.

293.

My girlfriend came home from zoo and was telling me how one of the small mammals had escaped.
It was Otter chaos.

294.

Although me and my ex-wife got divorced,
we still live on the goat farm together.
It's important to stay together for the kids.

295.

Me and my wife could argue until the cows come home,
mainly about how I'd managed to lose the Cows again.

296.

My wife says I'm too trusting.
At least, he says he's my wife.

297.

My wife says we need more garden Furniture.

I'm still sitting on the fence.

298.

My wife says my clothes make me look middle aged.

But still, it's the most comfortable suit

of armour I've ever worn.

299.

My wife went out to a fancy dress

party last night as a spider.

I woke to find her asleep in the bath this morning.

No idea what time she crawled in.

300.

I wake up every morning to find my girlfriend had painted my face black and put a big white line down the middle.

I just wish she'd stop badgering me.

301.

Someone's just said i look like The Fonz.

Happy Days!!!!

302.

My mate used to think he was clever by sneaking tubes of Sweets into the cinema by putting them down the front of his trousers.

Smartie pants.

303.

My mate is now self-identifying as a vampire.

I think he needs to take a good look at himself in the mirror.

304.

My mate asked me if I knew where his missing murder mystery board game was.

I didn't have a Clue-do.

305.

Wow! My mate just showed me his brilliant Invisible Man Impersonation and if there's a better impression out there, I haven't seen it.

306.

People say i'm not very good in arguments.

I'd have to agree with them.

307.

The 'Lumberjack of the Year' awards aren't being televised this year. Any idea why they've been axed?

308.

I'm at the airport and there are at least 3 electricians on my flight. Sparks are gonna fly.

309.

I've just received an acceptance letter from the World Taekwondo Federation. WTF!

310.

Etta James' full name is 'Estimated Time to Arrival James'.

311.

I can't believe they've cancelled that
TV show about Frankie Valli after 4 seasons.

312.

4 years I've spent at stage school and
I'm still no closer to being a stage.

313.

Every time I drive out of my local landfill site,
I leave a little tip.

314.

I am the worst person to play coin swapsies with,
Pound for Pound.

315.

I've set myself a 5 year plan to be more spontaneous.

316.

'Seldom' is a word I rarely use.

317.

I like doing multiplications, sum times.

318.

I won the Arm Wrestling World Championships single handedly.

319.

I make castration jokes, Willy Nilly.

320.

I only ever use George Formby antivirus, when i'm cleaning windows.

321.

I've spent most of today catching up with my marathon running friends.

322.

The beauty of Mount Rushmore before the carvings was unpresidented.

323.

The benefits of frosted glass are unclear.

324.

According to a survey, 1 in 4 hills are very steep.

325.

1 in 8 people in Russia are nesting dolls.

326.

When I was a gymnast, I was falsely arrested
over some assaults.

327.

I've never had a Splinter before.
Touch wood.

328.

I was taking a shower this morning
and HomeBase had me arrested.

329.

I've just written a joke about a lettuce and be warned,
it's a Little Gem.

330.

Yes!! Just landed the role of pantomime wasp.
Buzzin!!!!!

331.

Luckily this year he got the role as
'The front half of the panto Giraffe',
so at least he can hold his head up high.

332.

Cheap imitation Blue Tack.
I don't know how people put up with it.

333.

If anyone want to hear some jokes about oversharing.
I've got Piles.

334.

If I've said it once, I've said it a million times,
Always Repeat Yourself.

335.

I thought Lost Voice Guy was single.

Turns out he's spoken for.

336.

Trying to find an anagram for
'Sneaky Oats' is No Easy Task.

337.

For 3 years I dated the editor of 'Take a Break' magazine.

Never a cross word.

338.

Someone stole my local greengrocers van.

So far all efforts to get it back have remained fruitless.

339.

I was lucky enough to spend most of my
gap year working in Gap,
and I've got something similar
planned for Next year.

340.

Just got back from the antique shop.
Nothing new there.

341.

The medieval guitar shop next door
doesn't keep any stock on the premises
overnight because they're worried
about Luters.

342.

I asked my girlfriend if she could help me write my will.
She said "Sure, leave it to me"

343.

Bought my wife some neon contact
lenses for her birthday.
You should have seen her eyes light up.

344.

My wife turned our fridge off on the
wall before going to bed last night.
Not cool.

345.

I was going to tell my wife that I only use
fresh bait when I go fishing,
but i'm worried about opening up a big can of worms.

346.

My wife has got a face like a Scrabble board.
I still remember when I first laid I's on her.

347.

Last night I spilled my wife's bottle of Archers

on our dirty laundry by accident.

At first she was mad but everything's peachy now.

348.

My wife asked me to demonstrate my

Heimlich Manouevre technique.

I said " You must be Choking".

349.

I once bought my wife a bucket with a rope attached...

that went down Well.

350.

I massively overpaid for a big bottle of Listerene

earlier today and if i'm honest,

it's left a bad taste in my mouth.

351.

I recently bought some cheap deodorant from Isis, unfortunately I've now got the Police at my door investigating Terrorist Lynx.

352.

My local pharmacy has been out of flu tablets and Nytol for weeks.
I'm sick and tired of it.

353.

When I owned a dentist surgery, I never got on with the owner of the D.I.Y store next door.
We used to fight Tooth and Nail.

354.

All that time I spent teaching the kids how to make custard pies and they've just gone and thrown it right back in my face.

355.

I used to do the dry cleaning at the local nunnery.

I picked up a few dirty habits along the way though.

356.

There was this one time when my pants caught on fire.

Nobody believed me.

357.

I've got some great jokes about my kids being adopted.

But I can never find a good time to tell them.

358.

People used to say at school that I always

had to be the centre of attention.

But look at me now!

359.

At school I was turned down for the school pole vault team.

I never got over it.

360.

I spent 7 years of my childhood accidentally locked

in the hockey supply cupboard.

It was tough growing up in the sticks.

361.

When did I first become addicted to auctions, honestly
I can't remember.

I remember going once….. Going Twice!

362.

I keep thinking I can see Chocolate Eclairs out

the corner of my eye, just in my profiterole vision.

363.

I'm looking for someone to teach me
how to prepare desserts.
I'm free most days but cant make Sundaes.

364.

Dressing up as a green triangle before i go busking today.
That's the difference between a street performer
and a 'Quality' Street performer.

365.

The Old Man who puts cream in the giant eclairs at
my local bakery recently died and I got his Job.
I've got some big choux to fill.

366.

I'm on the look out for a new wrestling instructor.
A good one is surprising hard to pin down.

367.

I wasn't prepared for how expensive
spinal manipulative therapy actually was.
That set me back.

368.

There's no A&E in Basingstoke.
So it should actually be pronounced 'Bsingstok'.

369.

When I told the owner of my local library
that his chairs were far too lumpy,
there was an uncomfortable silence.

370.

Just got in from an awesome night out
with a lot of fellow Psychics.
It was everything i thought it would be.

371.

Been looking all over my Gran's house to find
the switch that turns off the storage heater.
I haven't found it yet but think I'm getting warmer.

372.

Etch-a-sketch have made me their
new head of development.
I'm looking to shake things up a bit.

373.

I recently learnt the welsh word for 'push' is 'lluq'.
I saw it written on a glass door.

ABOUT THE AUTHOR

Alf (real name Chris Leworthy) is a One Liner Comedian from North Devon, England.

He started comedy in 2015 performing at a few open mics around Devon and in 2016 he made it through to the finals of 'So You Think You're Funny' at the Edinburgh Comedy Festival.

In 2018 he auditioned for Britains Got Talent at the London Palladium and received a Standing Ovation from the Judges and the Audience.

In 2019, Alf was a finalist in the UK Pun Championships at the Leicester Comedy Festival as well as competing in the World One Liner Championship.

In May 2021 he start writing a Joke Book, turn to the front of this book to see how that went.

Printed in Great Britain
by Amazon